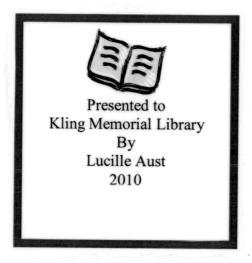

INSECTS
SIX-LEGGED ANIMALS

by Suzanne Slade   illustrated by Rosiland Solomon

Picture Window Books
Minneapolis, Minnesota

Thanks to our advisers for their expertise, research, and advice:

Celeste Welty, Ph.D.
Extension Entomologist & Associate Professor of Entomology
Ohio State University

Terry Flaherty, Ph.D., Professor of English
Minnesota State University, Mankato

Editor: Shelly Lyons
Designer: Lori Bye
Page Production: Melissa Kes
Art Director: Nathan Gassman
Editorial Director: Nick Healy
Creative Director: Joe Ewest
The illustrations in this book were created digitally and with pencil.

Picture Window Books
151 Good Counsel Drive
P.O. Box 669
Mankato, MN 56002-0669
877-845-8392
www.picturewindowbooks.com

Photo credits: page 22 (top row, left to right, and repeated uses),
iStockphoto/Le Do, iStockphoto/Sven Klaschik, iStockphoto/rusm,
Shutterstock/Michael G. Smith, iStockphoto/Le Do, iStockphoto/
Bogdan Dumitru, iStockphoto/Giuseppe Lancia, iStockphoto/Eric
Isselee, Shutterstock/Sebastian Duda, iStockphoto/Eric Isselee

Printed in the United States of America.

 All books published by Picture Window Books
are manufactured with paper containing at least
10 percent post-consumer waste.

Library of Congress Cataloging-in-Publication Data
Slade, Suzanne.
Insects : six-legged animals / by Suzanne Slade ;
illustrated by Rosiland Solomon.
p. cm. – (Amazing science: animal classification)
Includes index.
ISBN 978-1-4048-5524-3 (library binding)
1. Insects–Classification–Juvenile literature.
2. Insects–Juvenile literature.
I. Solomon, Rosiland, ill. II. Title.
QL468.S58 2010
595.7–dc22   2009004509

Table of Contents

A World Full of Animals 4

Insects at Home 6

Insect Bodies 8

Six Legs 10

Insects with Wings 12

Tiny Diners 14

Metamorphosis 16

A Hard Shell 18

Strange Insects 20

Scientific Classification Chart 22

Extreme Insects 23

Glossary 23

To Learn More 24

Index 24

A World Full of Animals

Millions of animals live on our planet. Scientists classify animals, or group them together, by looking at how the animals are alike or different.

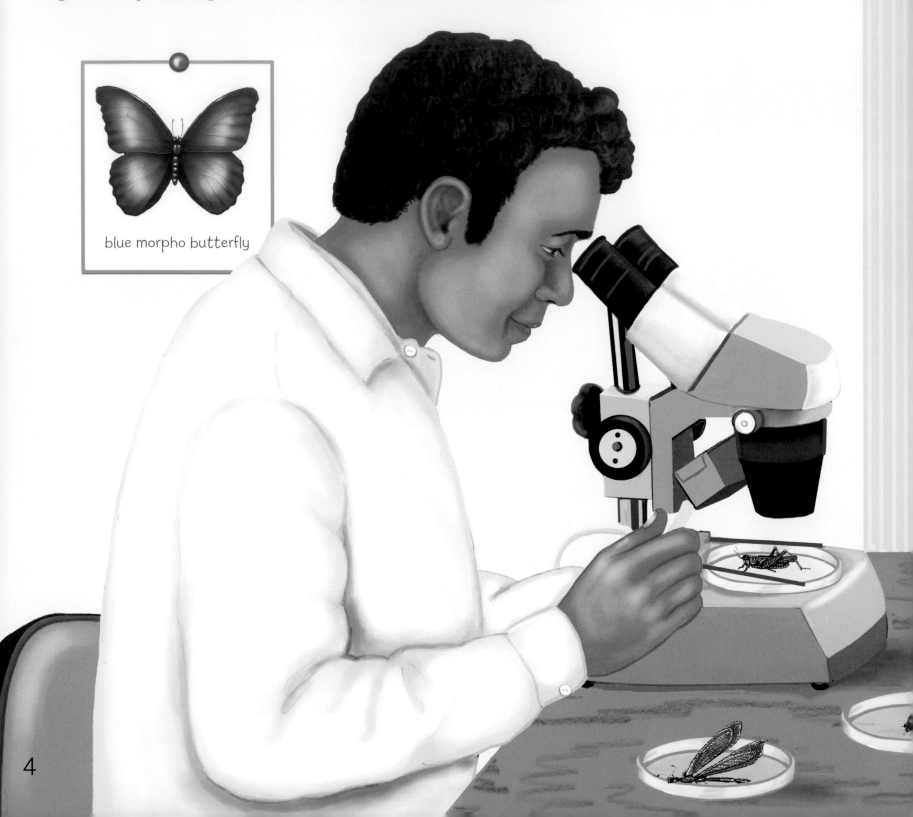

blue morpho butterfly

Six of the more familiar main groups of animals living on Earth are: mammals, birds, reptiles, amphibians, fish, and insects. Let's take a closer look at insects.

Diana fritillary butterfly

house fly

Nawab butterfly

grasshopper

dragonfly

goliath beetle

luna moth

More than 1 million different kinds of insects have been discovered. All insects have certain characteristics: They are cold-blooded, have three main parts of the body, have six legs, and have an exoskeleton.

Insects at Home

Insects can be found almost everywhere in the world. Temperatures reach more than 122 degrees Fahrenheit (50 degrees Celsius) in the dry desert where scavenger ants live. The Arctic beetle makes its home near the North Pole. Beautiful butterflies flutter near sunny meadows and flower gardens. Other insects, such as backswimmers and water boatmen, live in ponds and lakes.

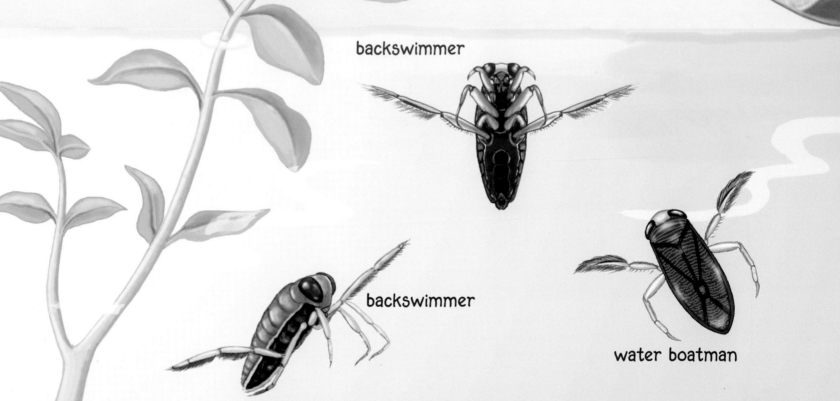

backswimmer

backswimmer

water boatman

Insects are cold-blooded. That means their bodies cannot make heat. When they need to warm up, insects rest in the sunlight. Arctic beetles, and other insects that live in cold places, have a special liquid in their bodies that will not freeze.

predaceous
diving beetle

water boatman

7

Insect Bodies

Most insects have three main parts that make up their body: the head, the thorax, and the abdomen. The head has a mouth, two antennae, and two eyes. These large eyes are called compound eyes, because they are made of thousands of tiny eyes. An insect uses its antennae to taste, smell, and feel things.

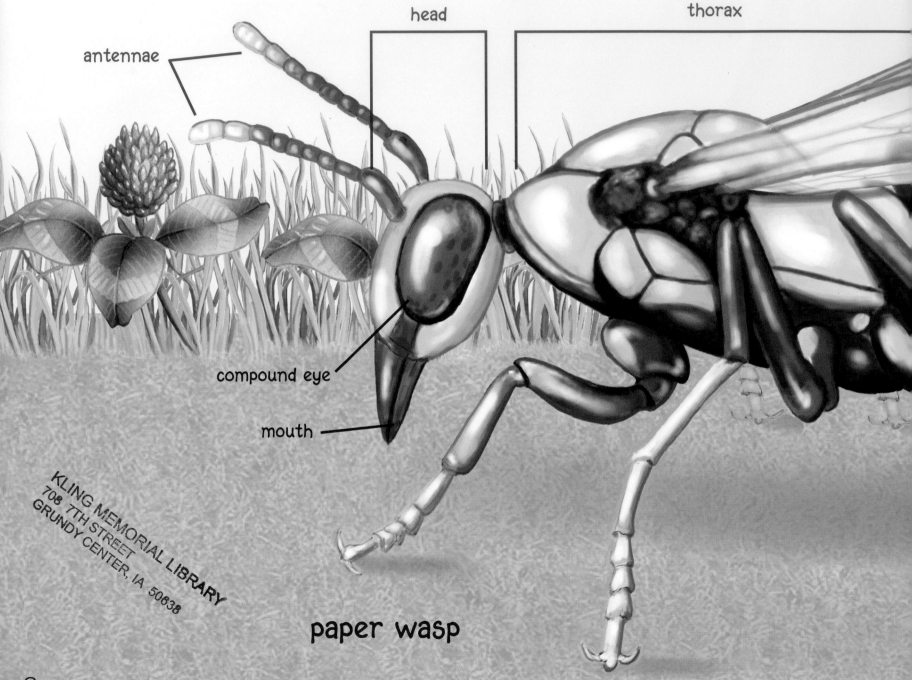

head

thorax

antennae

compound eye

mouth

paper wasp

abdomen

Insects breathe through tiny holes on their
thorax and abdomen. Like people, insects
take in oxygen and breathe out carbon dioxide.

Six Legs

You can tell if a small creature is a true insect by counting its legs. The legs are attached to the thorax. A grasshopper has six legs, so it is an insect. A bee has six legs, so it is also an insect.

grasshopper

honey bee

Some insects have special legs that do more than walk. A honey bee's hairy back legs carry a yellow powder called pollen from one flower to another. Flowers need pollen to make seeds. A grasshopper uses its strong back legs to make loud noises and to jump up high in the air.

Insects with Wings

Many insects have wings for flying. Insects fly around to find food or escape enemies. Wings are attached to an insect's thorax. Insects such as flies and mosquitoes have two wings. Insects such as cicadas and dragonflies have four wings.

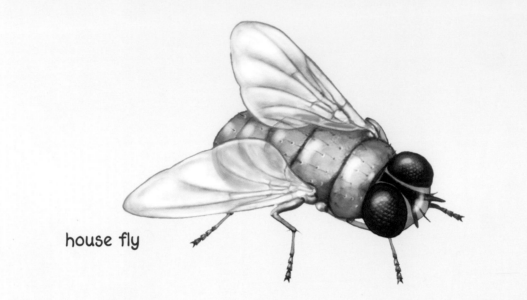

house fly

cicada

monarch
butterflies

tiger swallowtail
butterfly

blue hairstreak
butterfly

Butterflies are known for their large, colorful wings. Some use
their strong wings to fly thousands of miles each year. There
are more than 15,000 different kinds of butterflies in the world.

13

Tiny Diners

Most insects eat plants. They may dine on leaves, flowers, fruit, and even woody stems. Grasshoppers will eat almost any plant they can find. Some insects are predators. They hunt and kill other insects for food. A dragonfly often catches its meal while flying. It has strong jaws for chewing its prey, including mosquitoes and bees.

dragonfly

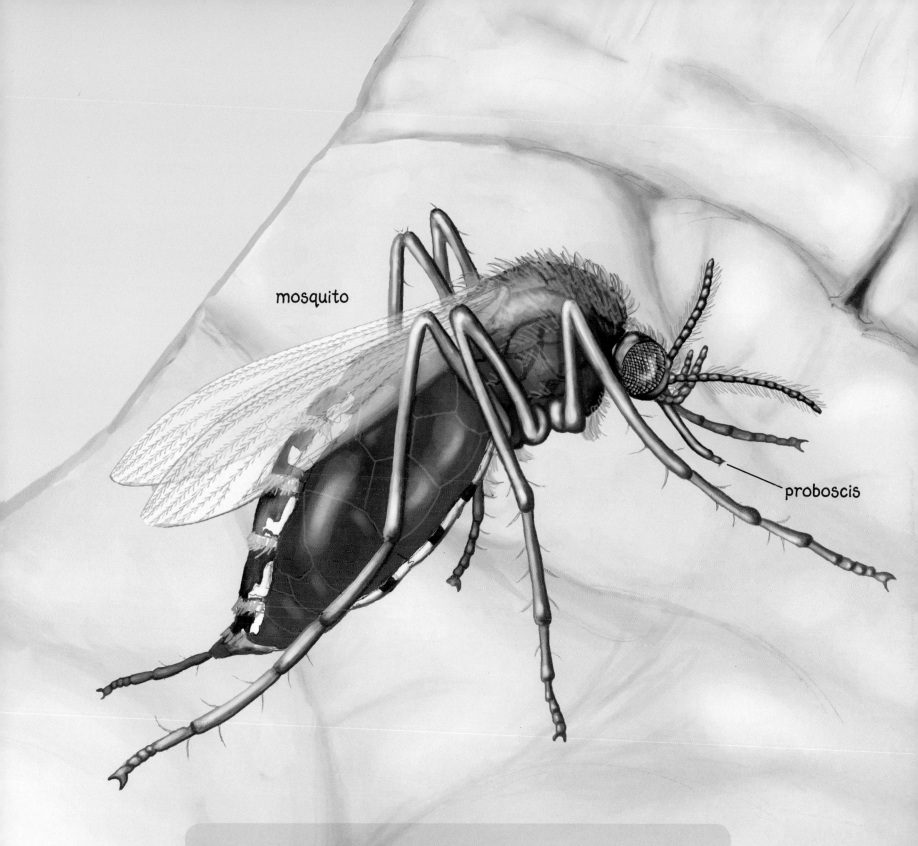

mosquito

proboscis

Many insects chew their food. Others have a special body part called a proboscis. The proboscis is shaped like a straw. Mosquitoes and butterflies suck liquid through a proboscis.

15

Metamorphosis

Some insects go through four stages of growth. This process is called complex metamorphosis. Butterflies, beetles, and ants go through complex metamorphosis. An adult lays eggs. Tiny insects called larvae come out of the eggs. As a larva grows, it sheds its tight outer skin. When it stops growing, a larva turns into a pupa. A pupa makes a covering around its body. Then it goes through amazing changes inside the covering to become an adult.

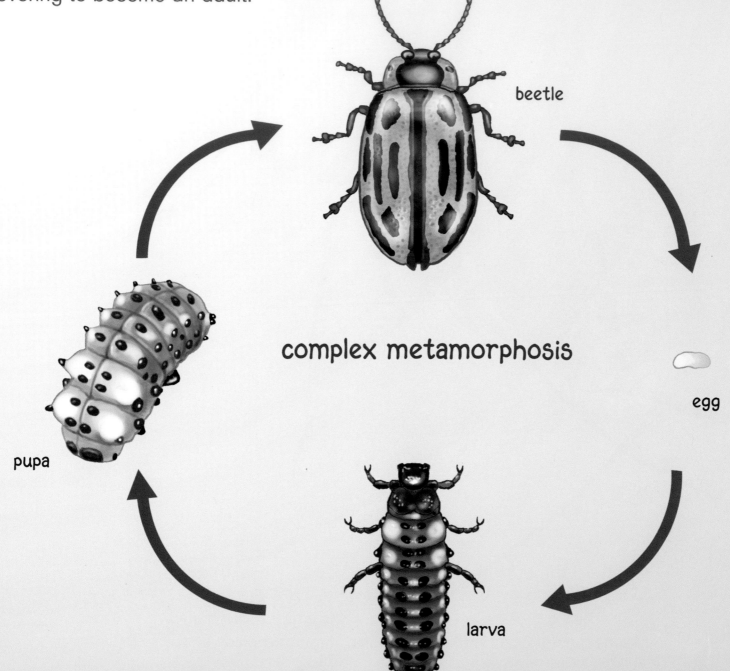

beetle

complex metamorphosis

egg

pupa

larva

Gradual metamorphosis is another way some insects grow into adults. Grasshoppers and dragonflies go through gradual metamorphosis. During this process, insects go through three stages of growth. An adult lays eggs. Tiny insects called nymphs come out of the eggs. A nymph sheds its outer skin several times. It also grows wings before becoming an adult.

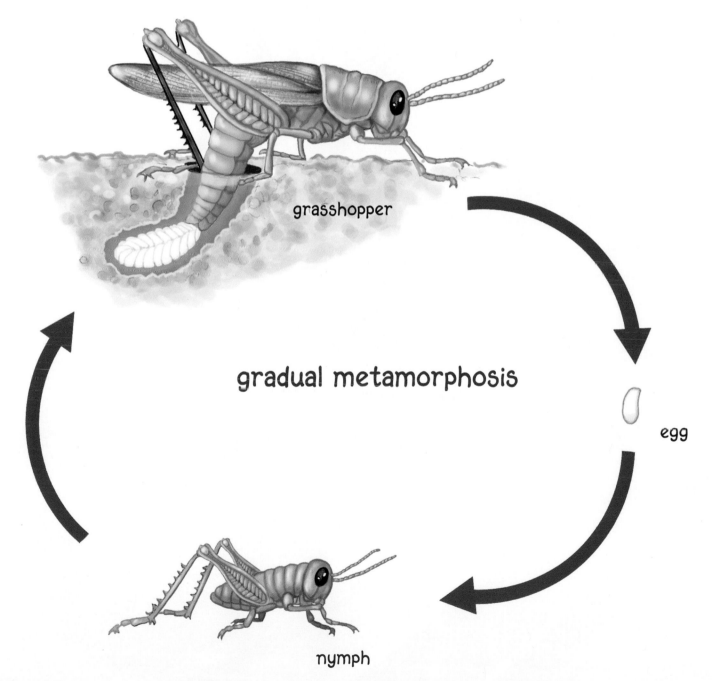

grasshopper

gradual metamorphosis

egg

nymph

A Hard Shell

Insects do not have bones to support their body from the inside. Instead, they have a hard shell on the outside of their body. This outer shell is called an exoskeleton. An exoskeleton protects insects. Some insects, such as ladybugs, have bright, colorful shells.

ladybug

adult

pupa

As an insect grows, its hard exoskeleton does not get bigger. A growing insect sheds its tight exoskeleton. Then a new, soft shell is uncovered. In time, this soft exoskeleton will harden.

Strange Insects

All insects are interesting. But some are stranger than others. A small beetle called a bombardier squirts dangerous liquid heated to 212 degrees Fahrenheit (100 degrees Celsius) when scared!

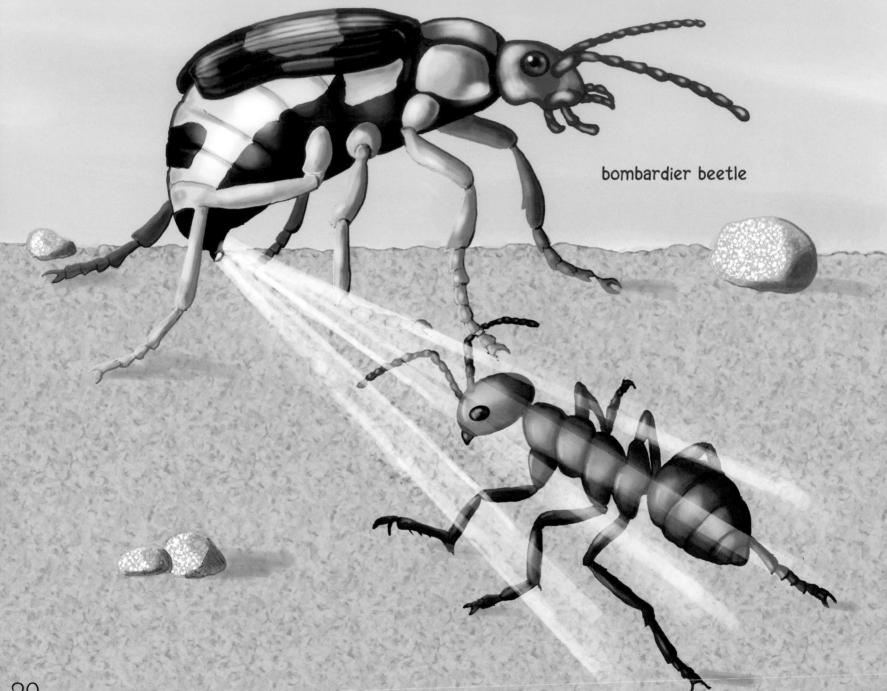

bombardier beetle

The 17-year cicada stays underground for 17 years. It comes out only weeks before it dies. The spittlebug blows a pile of bubbles around itself to hide from enemies.

spittlebugs

Scientific Classification Chart

The animal classification system used today was created by Carolus Linnaeus. The system works by sorting animals based on how they are alike or different.

All living things are first put into a kingdom. There are five main kingdoms. Then they are also assigned to groups within six other main headings. The headings are: phylum, class, order, family, genus, and species.

Kingdom: Animalia

Phylum: Arthropoda

Class: Insecta

Order: Lepidoptera

Family: Nymphalidae

Genus: *Danaus*

Species: *Danus plexippus*

Monarch butterfly

Extreme Insects

Longest insect: A huge stick insect found in Asia measured a whopping 20 inches (50.8 centimeters) long!

Brightest insect: The fire beetle has three bright spots that glow all of the time. Two of these spots are near its head. The third is on the bottom of its abdomen.

Quickest wings: A fly-like insect called a midge can beat its wings more than 1,000 times in one second!

Smallest insect: The feathery-winged dwarf beetle measures only 0.01 inches (0.25 millimeters). That's a little larger than a grain of sand.

Loudest insect: The African cicada creates more than 106 decibels. A decibel is the unit scientists use to measure sound. A rumbling train creates 100 decibels, so it's easy hear a cicada's loud song!

Glossary

abdomen—the end section of an insect's body

antennae—feelers on an insect's head used to sense and touch smells; antennae is the word for more than one antenna

carbon dioxide—a gas that people and animals breathe out

complex metamorphosis—the process of insects going through four stages of growth

compound eye—a large eye made up of thousands of smaller, separate eyes

exoskeleton—a shell or covering that protects an animal's soft body

gradual metamorphosis—the process of insects going through three stages of growth

larva—the stage of an insect's growth between egg and pupa in insects with complex metamorphosis; larvae is the word for more than one larva

nymph—a tiny, young insect with gradual metamorphosis

oxygen—a gas that people and animals must breathe in to stay alive

predator—an animal that hunts and eats other animals for food

prey—animals that are hunted and eaten for food

proboscis—a long, slender feeding organ that looks like a straw

pupa—an insect's stage of growth between larva and adult; the pupa often has a hard casing around it; pupae is the word for more than one pupa

thorax—the middle section of an insect's body

To Learn More

More Books to Read

Hudak, Heather. *Insects*. New York: Weigl Publishers Inc., 2005.

O'Hare, Ted. *Insects*. Vero Beach, Fla.: Rourke Pub., 2006.

Pyers, Greg. *Why Am I an Insect?* Chicago: Raintree, 2006.

Internet Sites

FactHound offers a safe, fun way to find Internet sites related to this book. All of the sites on FactHound have been researched by our staff.

Here's all you do:

Visit *www.facthound.com*

FactHound will fetch the best sites for you!

Index

body, 5, 8, 9, 12, 16, 18
breathing, 9
cold-blooded, 5, 6
exoskeleton, 5, 18, 19

food, 12, 14, 15
homes, 6
legs, 5, 10, 11
metamorphosis, 16, 17

proboscis, 15
wings, 12, 13, 17, 23

Look for all of the books in the Amazing Science: Animal Classification series:

Amphibians: Water-to-Land Animals

Birds: Winged and Feathered Animals

Fish: Finned and Gilled Animals

Insects: Six-Legged Animals

Mammals: Hairy, Milk-Making Animals

Reptiles: Scaly-Skinned Animals